KreativeKenn: It's probably about you

Kennedy Nieves

BookLeaf Publishing

Presentation by *BookLeaf Publishing*

Web: www.bookleafpub.com

E-mail: info@bookleafpub.com

ISBN: 9789357211185

First edition 2022

DEDICATION

This book is dedicated to everyone I love and have ever loved.

ACKNOWLEDGEMENT

Thank you firstly to my family - both blood & chosen. I want to mention my poetry mentors Elle Hope and Ashley Vargas (AyeVee). These women have shown me the light of their path, given support and love which has continued to lead me to show up for myself and express my heart through poetry. Thank you for the support & love from my slam team / family - Spotlight. And to all of the other incredible poets and artists I have met in this community.

I want to acknowledge my city Las Vegas for always holding me down and showing love & support as well. The city of opportunity, self expression, chance, love and abundance!

I want to thank my younger sisters Grace and Felicity for contributing their beautiful art to this book's cover. I want to thank my amazing photographer Taylor Jean (@taylorjeanphotography on Instagram) for the photo of me on the back of this book.

Just know I couldn't have done it without you. Thank you.

It's 5:03am

I'm in love with the world at 5 o' clock
When the sun peaks over the mountain top
The light comes in chasing darkness away
The sky is colors of blue and grey
The early morning streets are silent as my
neighbors sleep
It's so quiet I can hear the morning breeze
The street lights dim as the sun rises slow
In the early stillness, I swear, you can feel the
grass grow
So silent I can hear my heart beat against the
inside of my chest
My breathe steady in and out
I'm sitting in the silence of new energy
No words said to me
 only my own thoughts to sit with -
I am affirming everything that is meant for me
Letting go of what's not meant to be
It's in these sleepy hours that I find myself most
awake
Soaking in humility,
Gathering strength
It's in these dead hours that I find myself most
alive
Creating poems and stories,
And planning out my life

Pure bliss, effortlessly happy
Whispering to myself "Good morning"

Rivers & Roads

rivers and roads
that make me wonder if I'm lost or exactly
where I need to be,
when I look into your palms
I see a map of intersecting roads,
roads of an interesting mind
the feminine divine
meets Masculine Divinity
and it feels like home if I ever knew one
when I look into your eyes
I see rivers going for miles,
and I get the feeling of being lost again
but being exactly where I should be
blue river veins run deep down your arms
reaching out to pull me closely
touching my body
giving me shivers
licking me wet like a river
making your body quiver
knowing you want me
well, lover, you got me

rivers and roads
down hands that grab my waist
to pull me close and kiss me long

to make love
blue river veins and red roads run deep down
your arm,
meeting the prettiest hands
touching inside me
grasping my neck
long fingers
delicately cross with mine,
our bodies met at crossroads
at such an intense intersection
my rivers flowing in your direction
exploration, fascination
submission
I want you,
you have me.

Stupidly Accurate Metaphors and More Unanswered Questions

I've questioned over and over
Why did you leave me
Why did you go
I investigate our relationship like a crime scene
Where were you the night of the 23rd
I dissect our love like a frog's belly
Scrutinizing over words exchanged and mistakes
made
If I never said that, would you be here still?
If I looked any closer at the details, I'd go blind!
Where in the hell did I go wrong?!
When I gave you my heart, you crushed it
You burned it
And blew the ashes at me
Callously, maliciously
Your cruel intentions
Your wicked ways
What is it about you the drives me insane
What makes me hold on
Why can't I let go,
Time is supposed to heal everything,
but my wounds are still bleeding.

When will I stop dealing with
All these feelings of
Reminiscent love

Stubborn Love

I always wanted to be right
We'd argue,
And I would never be the one to give in
Or apologize
And I made this to be the reason of our love's
demise
I blamed my pure stubbornness on everything
that went wrong
When all that went right had grew from my
unyieldingness
When we were hanging by a thread
It was my inability to give in that held us
together
In your darkest moments
I was the consistent light guiding you out gloom
When you almost took your own life,
I held your face gently between my palms
Your head resting at ease
And I demanded that you were you worth
everything,
That you were great enough to move mountains
I always wanted to be right
I was passionate about you.
I was obstinate about our love
Stubborn love,

I was right
I'll love you forever

My Worst Friend

You broke my heart in words like
"We should stay friends"
I questioned this proposal because we were
never friends in the first place
We were magnet drawn lovers from the very
start
I loved you when I first saw you,
I loved you even more when you showed me
your heart
We never had intentions of being friends
When you invited me over to watch a movie
I kept you in my visual peripheral
Stealing glances between intense parts of the
movie
When your eyes were locked on the screen
I wanted to kiss you so damn bad I could barely
breathe
When we finally did
Your lively lips gave me an entire existence
I must have known you in another life
You were my wife and we spent an eternity
together
I know we existed somewhere before
We were never friends and you know we never
were

friends don't make you fall in love and then
break your heart
they don't cackle at the sound of your crying,
your begging and pleading, and your voice so
pained it cracks at every other syllable
friends don't kiss you every day until you can't
live without it and then leave you and smile at
you anyway
friends don't build a life with you so far into the
future you know your wedding theme, your
kids' names and what kind of home you'll have
together
friends don't break every piece of you when they
have you in both hands
My best lover, my worst friend.

Lover's Cure

The secrets and wounds have been revealed
Past and regret has been laid out for me to see,
...
I understand why you've been so resistant to the
love I have given so easily
I stayed persistent
I stuck around because I knew you were hurting,
and needed healing.
...
I taste the pain on your lips
I'm kissing away every word that broke your
heart,
That killed your soul
And harmed your spirit
...
Kissing away your hurt and sorrow
You taste just like distress
My lips soothe your wounds
I'll kiss you until you're healed
...
Love you now
so you learn how to love yourself
I see right through you,
your over arrogance,

your over confidence is a disguise to the self
hate, because you don't think you're worthy of
love
So you say no one else matters except you
But I know you love me
And you don't want to end up letting your guard
down
Just for me to burn down your castle,
You spent too much time building a kingdom but
I'm here to take down the walls, until you feel
free
I'm here to love you in ways she never could
I'll be your broken hearted lover's cure

I never planned for you

Searching long for a lover to give me the
affection I deserve,
 I gave up bitter in rejection
 In people's lack of love but need of attention
 Giving my all and getting nothing back
 Giving up because of the time I wasted on
temporary people
 Nothing gold can stay I always remind myself
 Because if I don't I'll end up disappointed
 Faking like fools gold
 And I'm the fool who called her treasure
 Who thought we'd always be together
 Because she promised forever
 Love hard because my heart only loves heavy
 get attached
 then come crawling back
 letting go of wrong doings
 because I couldn't see that I deserved better
 Vision clear now,
 I see now that I deserve better
 And you are so much better than any lover I've
ever had
 I looked at you and knew that we were destined
to be
 something more than strangers

Resistant to open up,
But I feel at ease in your arms
And it's alarming to me that
You were someone I never planned for,
Never looked for,
And didn't even try for
You love me for my flaws and for the fucked up
parts of me
 that I just can't hide because I'm sick of living a
lie
 That I am like a rose
Beautiful but plenty of thorns
Come closer to get hurt,
 Is it worth it?
 Do I deserve you?
 I don't want to hurt you, but it's hard for me to
believe
 That you'll stay
Because whenever I count on someone they
always prove me wrong,
 And I'm trying to be strong
 For you
 to let go of what was never good for me
Can we just be where we are and let love
happen
 because every time I plan for something it never
happens,
 It's always canceled
 So let us be by chance,

By accident,
Spontaneous romance
Something to last because if we never plan for
it,
then we will always have time.

I am happy (sad) for you (me)

Trying to write pain into prose
I cant stop thinking about you
and I'm torn
I'm happy that you found love and peace
but I'm sad that the happiness wasn't found in
me
I miss kissing you
& I miss the moments where we just understood
each other
when we were best friends and lovers
and we never thought about anyone else
because we were too content to think about
anything else but
that present moment
I miss your mind and your soul
your tousled sleep and how your body always
found its way to me
losing count of kisses,
restlessness in waiting to see you once more
to be hugged by you
to be embraced into your sacred scent
to have been loved by you once
feels like the greatest blessing,
but like an endless curse

Gratitude to You, Dad

I know that there's nothing I can give you in this
world
 that could ever compare to the sacrifices you
have made in your life for me and my sister
The man you had to become,
how you shaped your life around us, for us,
found existence and reason in us,
with us - you have unconditional love,
 I know that you could've run,
Could've dropped the title of dad,
Barely call yourself a father
Rarely call, or just never at all.
 I've seen it all,
 I've seen it worse,
and I'm so thankful for everything you have
done,
so proud of everything you have overcome,

Buildings and places are temporary,
But with you
I'll always have a place to call home.

Thank you-- quite obviously but unstated-- for
half of my chromosomes.
For the freckles on my face from you

For my blood consisting of mostly coffee

Thank you for giving me this mind
That is your reflection
Able of much retention
Always eager to know more

Thank you for those small little gifts because
you thought about me,
Coffee cups, good luck charms,
a surprise with the Spider-man movie
That meant so much more than you know
More than diamonds
And more than gold

Playing songs through the car stereo
Singing loudly off key but not caring about what
anybody thinks

Thank you for teaching me the impact of words
How language can hurt
Words we had exchanged in bitterness and anger
Words that left your tongue and let my heart feel
the impact
Words that left my tongue before my brain knew
the impact

Dad, you taught me to be real and raw---like a
poet

Made of good intentions but just misunderstood
You've always given me the world

Thank you for teaching me the the rarity and
scarcity of loyalty
so I don't trust easy
but always stay trustworthy
Teaching me the importance of commitment so
that I never give in
Creating stubbornness and passion within
Teaching me that's there's no right or wrong only
choices,
To only cry when it really matters,
To never apologize unless I mean it
Voicing to me to try harder even when I'm
giving you my all
because you only want what's best for me
Pushing me to be better even when I'm moving
slowly

Found myself drowning,
I found faith in your strength
That there's light after darkness
That there's sun after the storm

Thank you for the longest talks,
You always use metaphors
usually about basketball
or some kind of animal

Testing emotional capabilities, mental
capabilities
You know, you told me I have unlimited
possibilities
You told me I will do great things

Thank you for childhood memories to daydream
in now
To hold close to my heart
To find gratitude that you found time
In the stress of life for me--with adventures to
Disneyland and San Diego Zoo,
Movie Theater daddy-daughter dates,
& rare snow days and learning how to ski
Until I was riding black diamond mountains
Thank you for teaching me to be fearless
And that the journey may be lonely,
but the top of the mountain has the best view.

Thank you for teaching me that it's okay to be
alone,
to be in love,
to be hurt,
and to learn,
and to move forward

Thank you for giving me a heart that loves
heavy

Even though it can hurt

Your heart of gold beating in me
It's good to know I'll always feel more,
Understand more

You say I look just like my mother,
But my mind it looks like yours
The labyrinth of complexity, compassion, and
creativity
I'll always see a reflection of you

I had to take the time to express gratitude to you,
dad
so tha Gratitude to You, Dad

I know that there's nothing I can give you in this
world
 that could ever compare to the sacrifices you
have made in your life for me and my sister
The man you had to become,
how you shaped your life around us, for us,
found existence and reason in us,
with us - you have unconditional love,
 I know that you could've run,
Could've dropped the title of dad,
Barely call yourself a father
Rarely call, or just never at all.
 I've seen it all,

I've seen it worse,
and I'm so thankful for everything you have
done,
so proud of everything you have overcome,

Buildings and places are temporary,
But with you
I'll always have a place to call home.

Thank you-- quite obviously but unstated-- for
half of my chromosomes.
For the freckles on my face from you
For my blood consisting of mostly coffee

Thank you for giving me this mind
That is your reflection
Able of much retention
Always eager to know more

Thank you for those small little gifts because
you thought about me,
Coffee cups, good luck charms,
a surprise with the Spider-man movie
That meant so much more than you know
More than diamonds
And more than gold

Playing songs through the car stereo

Singing loudly off key but not caring about what
anybody thinks

Thank you for teaching me the impact of words
How language can hurt
Words we had exchanged in bitterness and anger
Words that left your tongue and let my heart feel
the impact
Words that left my tongue before my brain knew
the impact

Dad, you taught me to be real and raw---like a
poet
Made of good intentions but just misunderstood
You've always given me the world

Thank you for teaching me the the rarity and
scarcity of loyalty
so I don't trust easy
but always stay trustworthy
Teaching me the importance of commitment so
that I never give in
Creating stubbornness and passion within
Teaching me that's there's no right or wrong only
choices,
To only cry when it really matters,
To never apologize unless I mean it
Voicing to me to try harder even when I'm
giving you my all

because you only want what's best for me
Pushing me to be better even when I'm moving
slowly

Found myself drowning,
I found faith in your strength
That there's light after darkness
That there's sun after the storm

Thank you for the longest talks,
You always use metaphors
usually about basketball
or some kind of animal

Testing emotional capabilities, mental
capabilities
You know, you told me I have unlimited
possibilities
You told me I will do great things

Thank you for childhood memories to daydream
in now
To hold close to my heart
To find gratitude that you found time
In the stress of life for me--with adventures to
Disneyland and San Diego Zoo,
Movie Theater daddy-daughter dates,
& rare snow days and learning how to ski
Until I was riding black diamond mountains

Thank you for teaching me to be fearless
And that the journey may be lonely,
but the top of the mountain has the best view.

Thank you for teaching me that it's okay to be
alone,
to be in love,
to be hurt,
and to learn,
and to move forward

Thank you for giving me a heart that loves
heavy
Even though it can hurt

Your heart of gold beating in me
It's good to know I'll always feel more,
Understand more

You say I look just like my mother,
But my mind it looks like yours
The labyrinth of complexity, compassion, and
creativity
I'll always see a reflection of you

I had to take the time to express gratitude to you,
dad
so that you know that I really do appreciate you.

I love you.

Luv,
Kenn

Questions and Doubt

I doubted our love,

Questioning like why

why did you give your love to another woman
why was i not good enough
why did you leave
why am i so broken
why did you talk about forever and always if it
wasn't true

Questioning like how
how is it that one person can affect another so
deeply
how do you hurt me still when you are not even
here
how did you move on so fast
how did you break my heart so easily
how many times did you say "i love you" and
not mean it
how many lies did you tell me

Questioning like what
what was it about me that made you stop loving
me

what did i do wrong

Questioning like when
when was the moment you didn't love me
anymore
when did i hurt you
when did you meet your next lover

Questioning like who
who caught your eye
who tastes your honey-sweet kisses
who did you find a home in
who do you love more

Infinite questions,
Relentless doubt

Did you even realize that you shattered my soul?
Did you regret losing me?
Do you ever think to call?

I've called you a rose, but there is so much more to you than that.

Rose, I have felt your petal soft lips
And I've seen your rosy cheeks after you cry
But I have also felt your thorns
Blood drawing thorns–
There to guard your heart from the pain that
previously lingered from your past lovers
You were scared
You were weak
You were afraid to be loved by someone with
unconditional love.
You wanted to show me your faults and
weaknesses so I would run
But I stayed.
I looked at your weaknesses like they were your
strengths.
I looked at your mistakes and I thought them as
the essential part of your being
Those mistakes made you who you are today
You wanted so badly for me to stop loving you,
but I looked into the windows of your soul and
told you that I loved you.

You showed me what darkness looked like.
When you'd shut out the light and let sadness
overcome you.
When you forgot about the sun's warmth and
love.
When you showed me the coldest parts of your
heart,
I still loved you honestly and passionately.
When you gave your affections to other women
and so longingly kept your words of endearment
a secret
Despite what I had discovered I loved you.
The demise of our love was because of those
thick thorns
Your thorns cut me when I was trying to soothe
the pain in your heart
But now you're gone, we're done
and all you left me with are scars,
Letters of words that once were true,
And broken promises.
"A rose by any other name would smell as
sweet"
Despite everything, you are still magnificent to
me
I could call you a rose
But there was so much more to you than that.

You're a new day

You are my sun,
 but even you can't make the darkness stay away
forever

My morning star, I'd love you if my heart would
let me
 I'd let you light my heart if only it wasn't so lost
 If it wasn't so dark, I'd find a way to be with you
easily

I'm trying to find release in your eyes
 Feel the warmth of your sunny personality
 Remind me even on the grayest of days
 the sun is still shining,
 still prospering

Morning has never felt so right
 Sunrises will always made me think of you
 Because you remind me that not all things stay
dark forever,
 let the thoughts that consume me
 wash away in the light you present- so intense
 That I can't even think to be sad when you're
around
 so sunny, baby, I never want you to leave

But like the sun you'll always leave to make the
moon shine brighter
To let darkness be what it is.
To find beauty in your absence so I only long
for you more.
Soak up the sun so I can remember you when
you're gone
The nights long
And thoughts linger
Thoughts dig deeper
Until I'm consumed
Until I've thought about everything wrong I've
ever said
and every action that
caused you to love me just a little less

Bask in the glory of the morning sun
Start fresh in the light of a new day
Forget all the sorrow of yesterday
And start over

Let your love fuel the fire inside me
Burn passion within
And begin
To love without limits and become brighter
To become resilient and to always rise again
Glow and grow and continue to exist
To persist
To let the light heal my heart

You are the light and the start of something better

LOVE x TIME

My first love called it bad timing. Like if we had met each other later in life, we could have loved each other better. She could have been a better person. I could have been my own person. Being so young my father was breathing down my neck that "I don't know what love is" Rooting deep fear into the woman i loved - so much so that she couldn't even muster his name. It's something we just didn't talk about.
So when I "moved on" I met someone who's smile made me melt and who kissed like they were creating art. But I got tired of being a secret and told her I wanted her to myself. "I love you but I just love him, too." Key word–too. There wasn't room for two. Called it bad timing.
So the next time I tried to love someone I really thought they were someone different. I hadn't ever craved someone so much. I wanted to know every inch of their mind, body and soul. They just wanted to know my body. Lost in romance, do I even know what love is?
Blamed on bad timing, all these faults with love. I couldn't be my fault, or theirs, was it

the Universe's or God's? Who's to blame? Even
with fault taken it's all still the same.
Then finally you. This time I wanted to love
you. Maybe because you were actually amazing
and treated me right. Maybe because I needed to
make sure my heart was still more than just a
beating muscle. You made it feel like love was
worth all the pain I had previously endured. This
time the time was right. I was ready to love. I
just wanted to know you. Really know you. Tell
me what you dream of, what makes your heart
soar, and your mind wander. I'm moving slower
than I ever have before and I just want to know
your heart before I know the rest of you.
Is it okay to take things slow?
"I've only got time"

Used to you (Habits)

We began in innocence and purity
We were young and inexperienced
White turned to red
And we continued in excitement and desire
And I craved you so bad that it burned
We began in love
We began in honesty
So let us end in it too
People become habits
Good and bad
You were always there
You embedded yourself in my skin
What's yours is mine,
What's mine is yours
Do I really love you
Or was I just used to you?

A little honey goes a long way

Your name once left the taste of honey on my
lips
I had such a sweet tooth,
I couldn't shut up about you.
I'd tell everyone about wonderful and amazing
you were
How I'd fortunately found my soulmate so
young
My best friend,
My love
Honey-sweet memories
But then your vinegar vain
And the ways you hurt me
All of the repetitive pain
Broken promises and lies
when you said things like "forever and always"
I believed you foolishly
Because I've always loved the taste of honey

Soulmate—s

Perhaps soulmate is not defined as my one true
lover,
but as the people I'll cross paths with throughout
my journey,
to grow my knowledge about love and life,
to bring happiness offered with open hands
to create challenges to overcome
to give opportunities for self discovery
Through connection, building understanding
Exploring worlds outside my own minds
boundaries
Surrendering to love and letting go enough to
trust

...

Someone who touches my mind, body, & soul,
Teaching me lessons - making me a greater lover
and a better person

...

Someone whose heart beats sync with mine
Feeling like the timing is right but completely
losing track of time
lay and linger on your chest to feel the pounding
against my ear,
Your lunges, they fill with air, It feels too good
to be still

...
Stimulated conversations, much relation,
We talk for hours without thinking of what to
say next
We just flow

...
Lost in your eyes—they do say the eyes are the
windows to the soul.
Drawn to your passion and dreams,
Your entire existence,
You lose yourself in my soul
And i find myself in you
Never have you met a woman so certain
Never have you met a woman with a heart like
mine, eager to love you without collecting a
penny
Offering a penny for your thoughts
Holding space to speak freely
More myself with you than anyone else

...
You may not be here tomorrow, but I'll enjoy
today.
Soulmates exist to ignite passion and hold a
space for healing, to find people who match my
frequency,
It was a pleasure to soak in the auras of my past
lovers,
There's something to learn from everyone
Love is never a waste of time.

'To Do' list

An inked page with thin black lines
The title reads To Do
I write everything down
even if it is self-evident or habitual
Make bed
Brush teeth
Shower
There's a little box next to each task
I check off each and everyone
There is always something left to do
There has to be something left to do
I turned my sadness to busy,
And I'm so busy I can't tell if I'm sad
I have 'things to do' I tell myself
A whole list before there is time to cry
I thought about being sad—Clean room
I thought about crying—Grocery shop
I thought about having a breakdown,
But the movie starts at eight & it would be rude
to cancel
So instead of having a breakdown, I go out.
Then I go out again.
I forgot to be sad for days
I forgot to sleep for days, too.
Asking, why don't you smile like you used to?

I'm just busy.
I have plans at four
That doesn't leave a second to be solemn
A minute to mourn over our lost love
And how you did me so, so wrong
I'm lonely in my busy life.
I'm surrounded by people,
But I wish you were here.
Why is it that I write down everything I do,
I never wrote "Think about you"
But I still do.

Misdirection in Conversation

Conversation
By formal definition this word means,
"The informal exchange of ideas by spoken
words"
Conversation
"The exchange of ideas"
Meaning that one person gives while another
receives, and the other person gives while the
other receives.
A thought for a thought
Understand this concept,
In context to the relationship we have.
You tell me that we have these talks all the time
You say we have had "too many of these
conversations"
I let you know you're not talking with me,
you're talking at me.
You speak in one, infinite line, one narrow
direction,
I finally said what was on my mind
I've held my tongue, and held my tongue and
held my tongue,
and I can't any longer.
I spoke words that I crafted carefully, things I've
thought of a thousand times

I spoke words I carved into stone, but to you my
words are impermanent
Like I'd traced them in the sand, you let the
ocean wash everything I had to say away
You never listen long enough to hear me.
I speak on many plains,
on many lines,
in different directions,
and constant changes.
I'm here to listen,
but I'm also here to re-inform you
Of the misinformation you have about me
See, you have no idea what I'm thinking because
even if you do listen you're listening to respond
not to understand
I want to exchange ideas with you, but you
won't take mine, we can't have a conversation,
I've tried so many times
One straight line, one direction no other
I try to intercede but the infinite line won't
budge,
I try to create a new path, one that we can both
walk on together but you won't change
direction.
I'm stuck here looking through your tunnel
vision,
my life is not your decision. It's for me to
decide,

I can't walk on one line, I want to journey, I'm
wanderlust and I don't want to ever be stuck, I
thirst for knowledge, for enlightenment,
i can't be placed in a box and put a shelf, I don't
care to be looked like like a trophy,
if you can't talk to me, then you won't ever get
to know me. Let's take a journey.

Wanderlust in Your Eyes, Lover.

Do you think about me like I think about you?
 Thoughts consumed,
 Call it infatuation
 Like the sun does the moon
 I constantly chase you,
Like the sea does the shore I ask
 Why won't you stay
 But when you leave you
 Always come home back to me
Like spring chases summer
 Like fall chases winter
 I almost had you---but I always miss you.
 You're just like the seasons
 But give me a reason
 To stay

Say you can't see that I love you
 Do you think I'd open up to anyone?
 It's my pride that I'm putting aside just for you

I know I said some things unintentionally,
 I know I told you I didn't feel some kind of way
 I know I told you to go away
 But I truthfully can't be without you

I built a home in you
Roots too deep for me to leave
Somewhere for my mind to be at ease
A place where I can just be me
Maybe that's why I talk too much

Opening my third eye
 every time we speak
 Act like we're nothing
 Treat me like I'm something more
 I can't act complacent anymore
 Look at you when you're looking back at me
 Memorize your face
 Remember how your voice vibrates
 Soak in your scent that I'm always lost in,
drawn to
 I hope you'll stay
 But like everyone else you'll leave too

Tell me something real
 I'm trying to feel
 The more I try the less I feel
 Think about you even when dreaming
 Hold on to our past because I love what we
were
 How you made me feel
 How you make me feel
 Still..

You hold out because you're scared or
something
 Try to figure you out but wow you are
something

Our constellations were never meant to cross
paths
 I swear I'd rearrange the sky just to be closer to
you
 The universe and nothing less for you

Giving you my all
 While you give me enough to make me want to
stay
 Peel away your layers until we're at your heart's
core
 I meant when I said you were made for
something more

Explore the labyrinth of your mind
 Like I have time for puzzles
 But it's really you that has me puzzled
 And I'm struggling in between friends and
something more
 Do I mean something
 Or nothing
 or everything to you?

I never meant to find home in someone who
didn't love me too
 But a gypsy wanders and rests easily in the
arms of the wounded
 And in those in need of unconditional love
 Those who sin but need forgiveness
 But need accountability and direction
 I know you just wanted attention
 But I really loved you.

I'm yours

Stay inside me
Deeper longer
Pour honey down my throat
Wrap your fingers around my neck
And choke me
Hold your hand around me
Look at me like I am yours.
Know that I want you more than oxygen
Submission - I'm giving my body to you
You lick me until I'm at my peak
Fuck me until I'm screaming your name
This is all for you
my body against your skin
I know your heart and everything within
You are so much more than a body
It was never just about the sex but I lusted for
your lovely lips
Your words they drew me in
The way you smell invigorates me
Your body was more to me than just flesh and a
fuck
That night we made love
Look you in the eyes when you're inside me
Excite you
Revive me

Both breathing deeper
Make promises you know you'll never keep
while I'm wet by the touch of you
You say my name
I hold my breath
Then in a soft moan against my ear
I whisper, "Im yours"

Vulnerability Royalty

To be vulnerable is to be brave,
A transparent warrior fighting demons inside my
head,
Having battles
That leave me to pull the blankets over my face
To pretend that sleeping the day away will erase
the gloomy gray overhead like the sun does with
ease
Self-affirmations like
I will seize the day with confidence and poise
I will conquer the storm
I am like a sunflower, always facing the sun
Vulnerable so I can belong,
Tear down walls so I can love

To struggle is not a sign of weakness
Vulnerability Royalty
Wear my softness like a crown
Queen of openness
of exposing my emotional state
with nothing left
of pulling my ribs out of their cage
Showing my heart for the world to see
Vulnerable to your touch
Vulnerable to your lips

To your love
To the rush inside my body when you feel on me
when you're inside me
My body trembles when your lips brush against
my ear
Telling secrets like kindergarten lovers

I can't help but to reach out and touch
Especially when you tell me that everything is
mine
Well, the world is ours for the taking
and I need you so much more than your body
Tell me that you want me
because I need reassurance
I don't need the re-occurrence
of more time wasted and another heartbreak
If my heart breaks, it will surely shatter
and I want to experience life in the deepest of
ways
so being vulnerable, with you lover is the only
chance
I want to memorize every detail on your face
with my fingertips,
so that even if I go blind, I'll know it's you.
I listen to your voice like my favorite song,
Learn every word so I'll know what you'll say
even before you speak
Keep my roots deeply planted,

but let my vines grow with yours.
Like pages in a book, open up and get to know
me
Read every chapter, every page, every sentence
Know the details are what makes me different
Write poetry about you in metaphors and
limericks
Know writing is exposing,
open my heart to be tender like rose petals
Before a flower blooms, and opens herself up to
the world
Exposition, without much resistance
she blossoms and grows
Sunflower Queen,
Storm fighting beast,
Don't ever tell me that being open makes you
weak,
Because I've never been so beautiful,
I've never felt so free
Vulnerability Royalty

Printed in the USA
CPSIA information can be obtained
at www.ICGtesting.com
CBHW070113220924
14609CB00019B/1292